Technology Timelines

TELEPHONES
AND
MOBILES

W
FRANKLIN WATTS
LONDON • SYDNEY

Franklin Watts
This edition published in 2017 by
The Watts Publishing Group

Copyright © 2014
Brown Bear Books Ltd

Author: Tom Jackson
Designer: Lynne Lennon
Picture Researcher: Clare Newman
Children's Publisher: Anne O'Daly
Design Manager: Keith Davis
Editorial Director: Lindsey Lowe

ISBN: 978-1-4451-3581-6
Dewey no. 384.5'3'09

Printed in China

MIX
Paper from
responsible sources
FSC® C104740
www.fsc.org

Franklin Watts
An imprint of
Hachette Children's Group
Part of the Watts Publishing Group
Carmelite House
50 Victoria Embankment
London EC4Y 0DZ

www.hachette.co.uk
www.franklinwatts.co.uk

Note to parents and teachers concerning
websites: In the book every effort has been
made by the Publishers to ensure that
websites are suitable for children, that they
are of the highest educational value, and that
they contain no inappropriate or offensive
material. However, because of the nature of
the Internet, it is impossible to guarantee that
the contents of these sites will not be altered.
We advise that Internet access is supervised
by a responsible adult.

Picture Credits

The photographs in this book are used by permission and
through the courtesy of:

Key: b = bottom, c = centre, l = left, r = right, t = top.

Front Cover: tr, ©Adrio Communications Ltd/Shutterstock; cl,
©James Steidl/Shutterstock; bl, ©Maxx-Studio/Shutterstock;
br, ©Lawrence Roberg/Shutterstock
1, ©Maxx-Studio/Shutterstock; 4tr, ©Anneka/Shutterstock;
4bl, ©Ostill/Shutterstock; 5t, ©Stokkete/Shutterstock; 5b,m
©U.S. Navy/U.S. Department of Defence; 6b, ©Andersphoto/
Shutterstock; 6-7, ©Wikipedia; 7cr, ©photos.com/Thinkstock;
7b,©Wikipedia; 8b, ©iStock/Thinkstock; 8-9, ©photosobjects.
net/Thinkstock; 9cr, ©markjb/Shutterstock; 9b, ©Wikipedia;
10b, ©Everett Collection/Shutterstock; 10-11, ©Wikipedia;
11tr, ©Wikipedia; 11c, ©Library of Congress; 12b, ©Gary
Blakeley/Shutterstock; 12-13, ©Filipe B. Varela/Shutterstock;
13tr, ©iStock/Thinkstock; 13bl, ©RT Images/Shutterstock;
13br, ©Bob Orsillo/Shutterstock; 14b, ©Dja65/Shutterstock;
14-15, ©Lawrence Roberg/Shutterstock; 15cr, ©Wikipedia;
15b, ©iStock/Thinkstock; 16b, ©Bluehand/Shutterstock; 16-
17, ©H. Armstrong Robert/Classic Stock/Corbis; 17ct, ©Pixel
4 Images/Shutterstock; 17bl, ©Ablestock/Thinkstock; 17br,
©Wikipedia; 18b, ©Alexey D. Vedernikov/Shutterstock; 18-
19, ©Stockbyte/Thinkstock; 19b, ©Stillfx/Shutterstock; 20bl,
©Disc Pictures/Shutterstock; 20bt, ©Stockbyte/Thinkstock;
20-21, ©iStock/Thinkstock; 21b, ©Wikipedia; 22-23t,
©iStock/Thinkstock; 22-23b, ©iStock Editorial/Thinkstock;
23cr, ©Nikita Chisnikov/Shutterstock; 23br, ©David Pereiras/
Shutterstock; 24b, ©Wikipedia; 24-25, ©Multi-bits/The
Image Bank/Getty Images; 25cr, ©Wikipedia; 25bl, ©iStock/
Thinkstock; 25br, ©iStock/Thinkstock; 26, ©Coprid/
Shutterstock; 26-27, ©Joeseer/Shutterstock; 27tr, ©Rangizz/
Shutterstock; 27br, ©Scyther 5/Shutterstock; 28bl, ©iStock/
Thinkstock; 28-29t, ©Egorov Artem/Shutterstock; 28-29b,
©iStock/Thinkstock; 29tr, ©Boeing.

Brown Bear Books has made every attempt
to contact the copyright holder.
If you have any information please contact
licensing@brownbearbooks.co.uk

Contents

Introduction

At the touch of a button, a modern telephone can be used to talk to another person just about anywhere on Earth. We could also use it to send pictures and written messages – and even see the face of the person we are talking to. All this technology, which can fit into one pocket-sized gadget, did not exist 150 years ago. Back then communication was a great deal slower.

«A DIFFERENT VIEW»

MARATHON

Today, marathons are long-distance running races, but the first one was run to send a message. In 490 BCE, the Greeks won a battle at a town called Marathon. Pheidippides, a messenger, ran 42,195 km all the way to Athens with the news. This has been the distance of every marathon ever since.

Sealed letters

Until the 1800s, most communication was by letter. To ensure a letter was not read until it arrived at its destination, it was sealed with wax by the sender. The sender pressed down the soft wax with a ring or other personal object to show who it was from.

Code down a wire

The telegraph was invented in 1837. It sent written messages by wire. Tapping a key switched an electric current on and off to create coded electrical signals for every letter of the alphabet.

Waving flags

Brightly coloured flags are still used to send messages between ships using a code called semaphore. A signalman holds two flags in specific positions that represent a letter or number and spells out words to anyone who can see him from onboard the other ship. At night, the flags are replaced with glowing sticks.

Connecting

In March 1876, the American inventor Alexander Graham Bell made the first telephone call to his assistant: 'Watson, come here! I want to see you.'

A voice, like any sound, is a vibration in the air. Bell's telephone converted those vibrations into an electrical signal – and then back into sound.

Large box telephone

This early telephone was built by Bell in November, 1876. It used magnets to make an electric current vibrate like a sound wave. The current was sent from one telephone by wire to a second telephone, where it electrified the magnet, making its magnetic field rise and fall with the signal. The magnet pushed and pulled on a metal disk, which vibrated the air and recreated the sound of a voice.

CONNECTORS were attached to wires, which sent the signal to another telephone.

A HEAVY WOODEN BASE kept the phone still to reduce unwanted vibrations.

A MAGNET converted the vibrations of the metal disc into an electrical signal.

TIMELINE

1667
String telephone
English scientist Robert Hooke shows that sound waves can travel along a tight wire. A tin can telephone (right) works using this system.

1849
Talking telegraph
Antonio Meucci, an Italian inventor, experiments with electric shocks used to treat stiff joints. He uses them to transmit a voice signal into the body, so it can be picked up by the ears.

A METAL DISK behind the mouthpiece vibrates when the sound of a voice hits it.

THE MOUTHPIECE is also the speaker. A signal arriving from another phone makes the metal disc inside it vibrate, producing a sound.

ALEXANDER GRAHAM BELL

Alexander Graham Bell made many demonstrations of his telephone (A), holding conversations with his assistant Thomas Watson back at the laboratory (B). Bell answered the telephone by saying 'Ahoy!' Another American inventor, Thomas Edison, suggested using 'Hello!' At the time, hello was not a common greeting but was used simply to attract attention.

1861
Telephon
German Johann Reis transmits the phrase 'The horse does not eat cucumber salad', with a device named the 'telephon'.

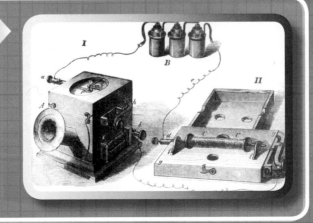

1876
First telephone?
American Elisha Gray designs a telephone that uses a water-filled microphone. He patents it on the same day as Alexander Graham Bell's telephone design.

Making Calls

In the early days of telephone calls, two telephones had to be plugged together by human operators working at a telephone exchange.

Telephone lines connected to a switchboard at the nearest exchange. You gave the name of the person you wanted to speak to and the operator would connect your line to theirs by plugging in a wire. When they got wires tangled and made a wrong connection it was called a 'crossed line'.

Wall telephone

From 1890 telephones used a microphone invented by American Thomas Edison. The microphone is made from two electrified plates with carbon granules in between. Sounds vibrate the granules and that makes the current running through the plates rise and fall in the same pattern, creating an electrical signal.

A HOOK held the earpiece when the telephone was not in use. 'Hanging up', after a call, opened the line so that it was ready to receive the next connection.

TIMELINE

1880s

Network

The first telephone companies begin to build networks of telephone lines in Europe, Australia and North America.

ELECTRIC BELLS rang when when another telephone made a connection.

A HANDLE on the side (not shown) was turned to sound a bell at the telephone exchange.

A HINGE allowed the mouthpiece to be moved out of the way when the telephone was not being used.

BOX CAMERA

Many of today's telephones also work as cameras. Photography had been invented in the 1830s, and in 1888 the first pocket camera was produced by the Kodak company. It was a box with a lens that focused images onto a roll of light-sensitive, see-through film.

THE MICROPHONE behind the mouthpiece was filled with granules of carbon. These wobbled around when sound hit them.

THE EARPIECE had a loudspeaker that works in the opposite way to a carbon microphone, turning an electrical current into the sound of a voice.

1888

Radio signal

Heinrich Hertz (right) builds a machine for sending and receiving radio waves. The frequencies used to tune radios today are measured in units called hertz (Hz) in his honour.

1897

'Wireless telegraph'

Guglielmo Marconi builds a test centre on the Isle of Wight, England, for sending messages by radio, or 'wireless telegraph'.

Wireless

In the early 1900s, a form of long-distance wireless communication was developed. It sent signals as radio waves.

THE TRANSMITTER was a large valve. It connected to a tall aerial that gave out radio waves.

Early wireless sets sent messages as pulses of radio waves. The transmitters produced a radio wave with a fixed amplitude (or wave height). In 1900, Canadian Reginald Fessenden invented amplitude modulation (AM), which meant the wave height could be varied. He then used an AM signal to transmit his voice.

Marconi radiotelephone

This radiotelephone from 1914 could transmit Morse code or voice conversations. It took a signal from a microphone and converted it into an AM radio signal, which could be picked up 50 km away. These devices were used mainly on ships.

CONDENSERS boosted, or amplified, the weak electrical signals so they could be converted into sounds.

TIMELINE

1900s

Automatic exchange

A system for connecting local calls automatically is invented. Exchanges staffed by human operators (right) are still needed to connect long-distance calls.

1904

Disconnections

There are three million telephones in North America. They are operated by rival telephone companies so half of them cannot connect to the other half!

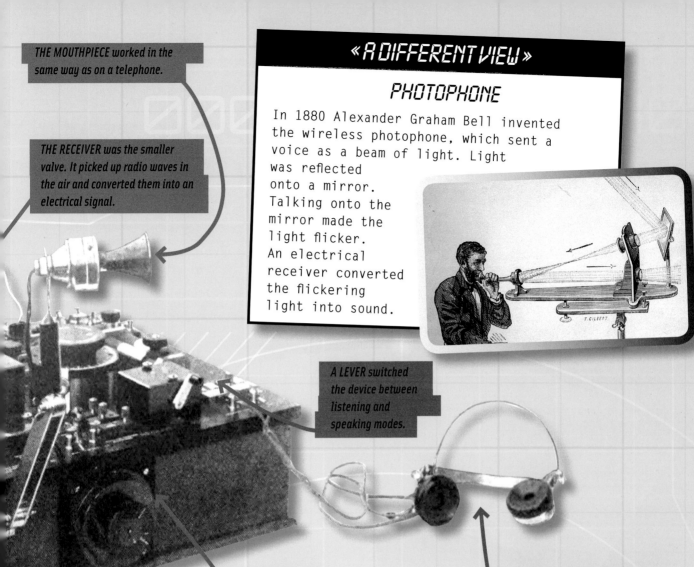

THE MOUTHPIECE worked in the same way as on a telephone.

THE RECEIVER was the smaller valve. It picked up radio waves in the air and converted them into an electrical signal.

A LEVER switched the device between listening and speaking modes.

A DIAL was used to tune the receiver to pick up the right signal.

HEADPHONES converted the signals received – either a voice or Morse code – into sound.

1912
Call for help
A Marconi radio on the RMS *Titanic* sends out one of the first maritime distress calls as the ship sinks. The signal alerted nearby ships to the disaster.

The World.

GREAT TITANIC SINKS; MORE THAN 1,500 LOST;
866 WOMEN AND CHILDREN KNOWN TO BE SAVED;
SCORES OF NOTABLES NOT ACCOUNTED FOR

LIST OF THE KNOWN SAVED

1915
Transatlantic message
The first voice message is sent across the Atlantic Ocean from a radio station in Virginia, USA, to a receiver at the top of the Eiffel Tower in Paris, France.

Dialing Up

Telephone numbers were introduced to make it easier for operators to find connections. By the 1920s, telephones had dials for inputting the number and getting through without needing an operator.

For much of its history, the telephone had a rotary dial. Even today we still say that we are 'dialing' a number. The rotary dial was invented in 1904, but did not become common until 20 years later.

Rotary dial telephone

To dial you inserted your finger in the correct hole and rotated the dial as far as the 'finger stop'. Then you let go and the dial spun back, producing clicking sounds. This was the pulse dialing system, which converted each digit in the telephone number into a series of pulses, or clicks. The number 1 was one click, 9 was nine, while 0 was ten clicks.

THE LOUDSPEAKER was at the top end of the handset.

MOULDED PLASTIC called bakelite, a new invention at the time, was used to make the body of the telephone.

TIMELINE

1920
Telephone box
A national network of coin-operated public telephones is set up in the UK. To begin with the telephone boxes are white. The famous red ones first appear in 1926.

1926
Calling New York
A two-way telephone call between London and New York City is made using a radio system.

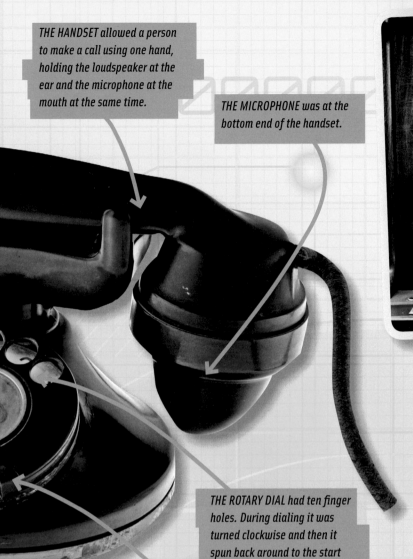

THE HANDSET allowed a person to make a call using one hand, holding the loudspeaker at the ear and the microphone at the mouth at the same time.

THE MICROPHONE was at the bottom end of the handset.

THE ROTARY DIAL had ten finger holes. During dialing it was turned clockwise and then it spun back around to the start again automatically.

THE FINGER STOP was as far as the dial could be turned.

« INSIDE OUT »

MULTIPLEXING

In 1910, an American engineer called George Owen Squier invented multiplexing. His system allowed one telephone line to carry several calls at once. The calls were merged into one signal to travel along main lines, but they could be split up again at the next exchange.

1937
Calling for help
The first emergency number – 999 – is introduced in the UK to call for police, fire brigade or medical help (right).

1940s
Walk and talk
Hand-held two-way radios (right) are used by American soldiers during World War II (1939–45). They become known as 'walkie talkies'.

Punching Numbers

Today's telephones are dialed using buttons. This system is called tone dialing, or 'touch-tone'. It was first introduced in **1963**.

In the 1950s, it was not possible to make a direct telephone call outside of your town. To call another city, let alone another country, you had to be put through by several operators. 'Touch-tone' dialling was designed to put an end to these complications. It made it easier to dial complex numbers complete with area codes, which directed the call automatically to wherever in the world it needed to go.

Touch-tone phone

The phone had 12 buttons. Each one produced a tone with a specific note, so phone numbers were transmitted as unique sets of tones.

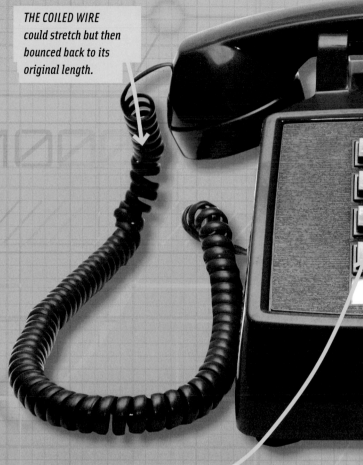

THE COILED WIRE could stretch but then bounced back to its original length.

THE STAR KEY is used to input codes that check the line or transfer a call.

TIMELINE

1950s
TV broadcasts
Television sets become more common. They receive pictures and sounds from a powerful radio signal broadcast across a wide area.

1956
Laying cable
The first telephone cable is laid across the Atlantic Ocean (right). The TAT-1 line, running between Scotland and Canada, can carry 36 calls at once.

A DIALING TONE became standard in the 1960s. It showed that the line was ready to make a call.

LETTERS were included on keys so people could dial words as well as numbers.

THE HASH KEY, or 'number sign' is used like an 'enter' button when inputting codes and other information.

EACH BUTTON produced a tone of a specific note, or pitch.

1963
Instant pictures
The Polaroid camera is introduced. It can produce colour photographs on paper within a minute or two. Before this, photographs had to be sent to a developer before they could be seen.

1965
Satellite links
The first communication satellites are launched into 'geosynchronous orbit'. Each one stays above the same point on Earth's surface, making them ideal for transmitting signals.

Computer Network

In the 1960s computers linked by telephones were used by the military. A project to keep such networks working during a future war had an unexpected result: the Internet.

A connection is only as a strong as the line between the two handsets or computers. In 1964 packet switching was invented. This split computer files into small 'packets' and each one travelled through the network by itself. If a line was broken and a packet did not arrive, it was just sent again until it found another way through. This is the system used in today's Internet.

Modem connection

Computer files are sent down telephone lines as sounds produced by a device called a modem. This 1969 modem converted files into whining sounds that were audible to the human ear.

A NETWORKED COMPUTER can be used to control any device at the other end of the telephone line.

THE MODEM, short for modulator/demodulator, is where the computer connects to the telephone system.

TIMELINE

1969
The Internet
University computer networks in California are connected by telephone lines. This is the start of a 'network of networks' – or the Internet.

1973
Mobile phone
Cellular telephones (right) are tested for the first time in the United States. They use a mix of radio and telephone technology.

1975
Scanning paper
Optical fax machines – short for facsimile, meaning 'copy' – (right) convert documents into telephone signals by scanning them with a light beam.

PICTURES, TEXT and other computer files can be sent along telephone lines.

EMAIL

Networked computers could send and receive electronic mail – or email. The first system was developed in 1961 but only worked for computers that were on the same network. In 1971 the @ style email address was invented, which meant messages could be sent through the Internet.

THE TELEPHONE sends computer files as sounds down the line and picks up sounds coming from other computers on the network.

EACH KEYSTROKE produces a seven-digit code (made of 1s and 0s). Text is transmitted as sets of these codes.

1981
Standard plugs
All British telephones start to use the same size of plug to connect to the line, as the world's telephone hardware becomes more standardised.

1982
Emoticon
The happy and sad face emoticons are used to signal moods in an email message for the first time.

Going Mobile

The idea of a communication device that everyone carried was once the stuff of science fiction. In the 1980s, a portable system was developed that combined radios with telephones.

THE ANTENNA, or aerial, sends and receives radio signals coming from the nearest cell tower.

Early mobile phones had one big problem –they were very heavy and therefore not very mobile. By the early 1990s, phones had become small enough to be practical. Mobile phones are also known as cell phones, because they connect to radio towers that cover one area, or cell.

A LARGE BATTERY made the phone much thicker than modern phone models.

2G mobile phone

In 1991, a second generation of mobile phone was launched. The 2G network was digital. The signals sent and received by telephones were a coded string of digits (1s and 0s), not a rising and falling series of sound waves as in earlier technology (see page 16).

THE SCREEN shows the number as it is being dialed.

FUNCTION KEYS give access to stored telephone numbers and voicemail.

TIMELINE

1988
Fibre optic cable
The first fibre optic cable is laid under the Atlantic between the UK and the United States. It can carry 40,000 telephone calls at once as a light signal sent through glass fibres.

1989
Getting online
Internet service providers (ISPs) offer connections to the Internet through home telephone lines.

1992
SMS
The short message service (SMS), or texting, is tested for the first time. It transmits short texts of 160 characters or less between phones.

CELLULAR NETWORKS

Mobile phones send and receive calls as radio messages. They communicate with the closest cell tower, switching to another as the caller moves. The cell tower forwards the call through the main telephone network.

A HINGED FLAP was opened to answer a call or dial a number. It contained a tiny microphone.

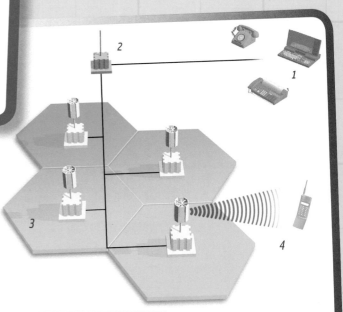

1. A signal is sent from a wired device.
2. The exchange directs the call to the cellular network.
3. Each cell tower picks up ID signals from all the phones in its cell.
4. A tower transmits the call to the phone.

1993

Bluetooth
A radio system is introduced so telephones, computers and other devices can connect and exchange data over a short range of a few metres.

1995

Internet calling
The first voice over Internet protocol (VoIP) service is launched. It allows people to chat via their computers rather than telephones.

Adding Pictures

During the 1990s, digital cameras were becoming more popular, replacing cameras that used film. It would not be long before cameras were added to mobile telephones.

LIGHT FROM THE SUBJECT travels into the camera through the lens and is focused on a layer of light-sensitive electronics that create the digital image.

A camera uses a light-sensitive surface to capture an image. Early cameras did this with flexible plastic film coated with chemicals. A roll of film could take up to 36 photographs before it had to be replaced. In 1975, the charge-coupled device (CCD) was invented. This was a light-sensitive electronic grid that produced pulses of electricity when hit by a beam of light. The pattern of these pulses could be used to create digital images – images stored as computer files rather than on plastic film. The technology was originally used for spy satellites and telescopes, but by the late 1990s, CCDs were being used in inexpensive digital cameras.

A LIVE PICTURE appears on the screen to help the photographer compose the image.

TIMELINE

1996
Caller waiting
The identity of the caller can be displayed on certain phones. A beep also sounds during a call as a signal that another caller is on the line.

1997
Call centres
It becomes common for customers to access services by talking to a telephone call centre (right).

THE COLOUR SCREEN uses a flat LED display, like on a laptop or TV.

Image in camera

Sharp image

lens

hole

object

TAKING PICTURES

The word camera means 'room' in ancient Greek. In effect a camera is a space sealed off from the outside world apart from a tiny hole. Beams of light entering the hole form an image on the opposite wall. Light-sensitive film or electronics then capture that image as a photograph. A lens focuses the light beams into a sharper image.

CONTROLS on the back of the camera can add effects, control the flash or switch to video mode.

A MEMORY CARD stores hundreds of photos, which can be reviewed on the screen or downloaded to a computer and printed on paper.

ISO

FUNC. SET

MENU

DISP.

1467

L

2000s
Broadband
High-speed Internet becomes available through telephone lines. The data is sent as high-pitched sound. A filter (right) at the socket cuts out this whistling noise so you cannot hear it.

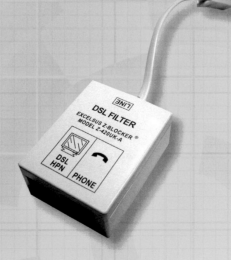

DSL FILTER
EXCELSUS Z-BLOCKER ®
MODEL Z-420UK-A

LINE

DSL HPN | PHONE

2001
Satellite phones
It becomes possible to make a call from almost any place on Earth (except the poles) by bouncing a signal off satellites, which then connect to the main telephone network.

Smarter Phones

A modern mobile telephone is known as a smartphone because it does a lot more than make calls. It is a small hand-held computer.

3G TECHNOLOGY allows the smartphone to send emails and access the Internet as well as to make telephone calls.

The early designs of mobile phones copied those of home telephones. They were a handset with a touch-tone keypad, earpiece and microphone. In 2007 the first smartphones changed all that. The keypad was removed and almost all of the device was taken up with a touch-sensitive screen. Making telephone calls was just one of many functions. To dial a number or send a text, the screen displayed 'soft keys' – a keypad or keyboard that appeared on the screen itself. This disappeared when the screen was needed for something else, such as to watch a video, play a game or read a book.

APPS APPEAR AS ICONS on the screen. Pressing an icon will launch the app.

PHYSICAL BUTTONS on the phone turn the phone on and off or return it to a start screen.

TIMELINE

2003

Video calls
Skype, a video call service, is launched. It sends pictures and sound between computers through the Internet.

2006

Accurate sat nav
The full GPS (global positioning system) signal is made available to non-military systems. Telephones are equipped with GPS technology.

2008

App stores
Games and other small applications, or apps, are made available to download straight to smartphones.

TOUCHSCREENS

Without a keypad, the smartphone is controlled by a touchscreen. This is made from two layers of glass with capacitors sandwiched in between and arranged in a grid. A capacitor is a device that holds an electric charge. Touching one of the capacitors with a finger or stylus pulls some of that charge away. This shows the phone where you are touching the screen - on a button or icon - and it changes the display accordingly.

9:30 AM

MESSAGES

CONTACTS

TIME

CALENDAR

MAIL

SETTINGS

TINY DIGITAL CAMERAS are on the front (and back) of the smartphone.

A SEARCH FIELD is used to look for things stored on the telephone. A 'soft' keyboard appears on the screen for typing words.

2011

Mobile music
The number of songs downloaded to telephones and computers outstrip CDs bought in shops for the first time.

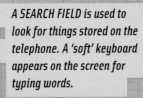

Video Calls

Nearly 90 percent of homes and offices in the UK have high-speed Internet access. These powerful connections make it possible to see as well as hear people during calls.

AN INSET SCREEN shows the caller what the other person can see.

By the 21st century, all telephone calls used digital technology. Instead of sending an electrical version of a sound wave, the telephone converted the voice into a computer file. Video can be sent in the same way. However, a video file contains more information than sound alone, and so it only works when both callers have broadband.

Tablet calls

In 2011 video calling became possible from tablet computers, like the Apple iPad. These devices have larger screens than telephones but are still easy to hold in the hand.

TABLET COMPUTERS, with larger screens than telephones, are ideal for making video calls.

TIMELINE

2012
Wireless charging
A wireless charging system called Qi (pronounced 'chee') is adopted as standard. It charges devices without the need for plugs by transferring energy from a coil in the charger to a coil in the phone.

2013
Smart watch
A wristwatch (right) that can make phone calls (the microphone is in the buckle), send emails and texts, and take photos and videos is launched.

THE CONNECTION for the call is made through broadband, Internet or the latest '4G' mobile network.

THE CAMERA can send a video of the person speaking, or be switched to show the surroundings of the person calling.

« A DIFFERENT VIEW »

AUGMENTED REALITY

The camera of a smartphone can be used to add extra layers of reality to the surroundings. This is AR - augmented reality; 'augmented' means 'made better'. The AR layer can show information about a landmark, it can let you see where your friends are in a crowd, or it can turn an everyday view into an exciting game.

Lake Helen, Florida   20.0 miles
For the high-altitude lake in Lassen Volcanic National Park, see Lake Helen (Lassen Peak)Lake Helen is a city in Volusia County, Florida, United

radius 31.71 mi.   GPS

WIKITUDE

Smart Watch
10:12
Saturday, June 10

2014

Selfie

A new word is introduced to English: A 'selfie' is a self-portrait picture taken using a smartphone – and then posted on the web for people to see.

Wearable Tech

The latest communications technology is getting so compact it can be worn on the body as a watch or headset. It will change the way we communicate all over again.

In 2014 Google Glass, the first headset computer, was put on sale. It is connected to the Internet and is controlled by voice commands and by swiping a fingertip on a touch-sensitive pad. Only the wearer can see what is on the tiny screen and hear the loudspeaker – which sends sounds right through the skull to the inner ear. The device can make telephone calls, display text messages, give directions and take a video of whatever the wearer can see!

« INSIDE OUT »

LITHIUM-ION BATTERY

Modern electronics are powered by a rechargeable lithium-ion battery. During charging, charged lithium ions are pushed into a crystal mesh. When the battery is being used, these ions are released to create an electric current.

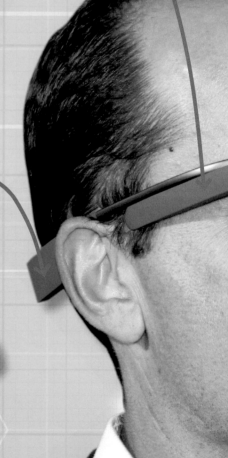

A TOUCHPAD on the side of the head is used to scroll the screen, take photos and answer calls.

THE BATTERY is behind the ear. It is smaller than the battery in a smartphone and only lasts a few hours before it needs charging.

LITHIUM ION BATTERY
Li-ion 3.7V 1600mAh
Charge limit voltage: 4.2V
Standard: GB-18287-2000
Production Date: 2009.12
Attention: 1.Do not approach the fire to avoid detonation
2.Do not disassemble the battery secretly.
3.Strictly prohibit short ciruiting when the
4.Please refer to the user handbook when the
battery need charging.

Li-ion

Zapping a code

Telephones can access services and information by scanning a square full of black dots. These patterns are called QR codes (short for 'quick response'). Each code has a unique pattern of dots, which is captured by the smartphone camera. Once decoded, it links to a website or app. If you are interested in something, just zap its QR code.

A CAMERA AND TINY SCREEN are positioned over the right eye. The camera takes a video of what you can see. Images are projected onto a tiny see-though screen.

THE 'GLASSES' do not have lenses – but can be fitted with them if required.

Digital wallet

Telephones can be used to pay in shops and transfer small amounts of money to friends. The phone has to be registered with the bank. It can then connect with a till to pay for goods. Another app lets you transfer funds to another person just by typing in their telephone number.

Future Communication

Today's communication devices allow people to speak to each other, access information from the Internet and send a message to thousands of people all at once. However, there are still a few barriers to communication that need to be fixed.

Communication technology is expensive and difficult to mend if it is broken in an accident. Future telephones will be much tougher than they are today. Also, technology will allow devices to connect anywhere on Earth and understand any language.

Auto translate

You can call anyone in the world, but you might not understand what they say. Computers able to recognise what a person is saying could then translate it into any language. In future, phones will translate any language into a computer voice that you can understand.

Flying antenna

Remote areas that do not have a cellular network could get coverage from fleets of drone aircraft. This experimental model has a body of an airship filled with helium and long wings like an aeroplane. It can fly for four days and could be used to connect with phones on the ground.

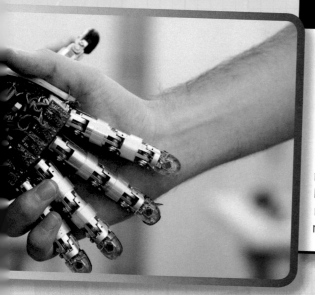

Flexible phones

Modern smartphones are quite fragile, and dropping them can be an expensive accident. New materials called organic light-emitting diodes (OLEDs) will make future gadgets much more flexible. They will bend not break if dropped and they could be designed to fold up to fit into a pocket. OLEDs can be made into any shape and will transform electronics in the future.

« A DIFFERENT VIEW »

TELEPRESENCE

While telephone means 'distant voice', telepresence technology lets a person appear to be in a place with you, far from where they actually are. The simplest method is to join in with a meeting or lesson via video screen. However in the future, telepresence robots controlled by a person far away may be common in schools and offices.

Glossary

2G Short for second generation. The 2G mobile phone network was launched in 1991.

3G Third generation. The 3G mobile phone network was launched in 2001.

4G Fourth generation. The 4G mobile network was first launched in 2006.

amplitude A measure of how high a sound wave vibrates.

amplitude modulation (AM) A method of coding a communications signal by altering the amplitude of the wave carrying it.

app A small application, or programme, used on a smartphone or other hand-held device.

broadband An Internet connection capable of transmitting large amounts of data.

cellular Meaning divided into cells, or small areas.

data Items of information, normally organised as numbers.

digital Something expressed as a code of numbers, or digits.

drone An aircraft with no pilot.

fibre optic A communications cable that sends signals as flickers of light.

frequency A measure of how often something happens. A radio frequency refers to how often the wave vibrates.

geosynchronous orbit A path of a satellite that stays above the same point on Earth's surface.

granules Small pellets.

icon A picture symbol.

ion A charged particle containing one or more atoms.

maritime To do with ocean travel.

modem A machine that lets computers communicate by telephone.

Morse code A system of dots and dashes used to code letters and numbers.

switchboard A device where several telephone lines connect.

telegraph A system for sending messages by electric wires.

Further Resources

Books

Alexander Graham Bell (Science Biographies), Catherine Chambers. Raintree, 2014.

Old Telephones, Andrew Emmerson. Shire, 2010.

Telegraph, Telephone, & Wireless: How Telecom Changed the World, Bert Lundy. BookSurge Publishing, 2009.

The Telegraph and Telephone (Great Inventions), Richard Worth. World Almanac Library, 2006.

The Telephone (Tales of Invention), Richard Spilsbury and Louise Spilsbury, Heinemann Educational Books, 2010.

What's Next for Communication? (Future Science Now), Tom Jackson. Wayland, 2013.

Websites

http://www.bitrebels.com/technology/the-evolution-of-smartphones-infographic/
The evolution of the smartphone.

http://www.mhs.ox.ac.uk/marconi/exhibition/index.htm
Museum of the History of Science at Oxford's online exhibition about the invention of radio.

http://www.corp.att.com/history/inventing.html
The story of the telephone as told by AT&T, the oldest telephone company.

http://www.bbc.co.uk/schoolradio/subjects/history/victorians/inventions/telephone
A short video about the invention of the telephone from the BBC.

https://youtu.be/qWUP9EigdjY
Some amazing facts about the history of the telephone according to National Geographic TV.

Index